SHORT WALKS
CORNWALL

NEWQUAY AND THE NORTH COAST

by Phil Turner

Barras Bay and Merope Rocks (Walk 6)

CONTENTS

Using this guide... 4
Route summary table 6
Map key 7
Introduction... 9
  Walking in Newquay and the north coast 10
  Things to see 11
  Travel 11
  Where to stay... 11

The walks

1.	West Pentire and Polly Joke	13
2.	Newquay	17
3.	Watergate Bay to Newquay	23
4.	Mawgan Porth and St Mawgan	29
5.	Park Head and Pentire Steps	35
6.	Trevose Head	39
7.	Padstow and Prideaux Place	43
8.	Little Petherick Creek	49
9.	Rock and Polzeath	55
10.	Pentire Point and The Rumps	61
11.	Port Isaac	65
12.	Camelford	71
13.	Tintagel	75
14.	Boscastle	81
15.	Bude Canal and coast	87

Useful information... 95

USING THIS GUIDE

Routes in this book

In this book you will find a selection of easy or moderate walks suitable for almost everyone, including casual walkers and families with children, or for when you only have a short time to fill. The routes have been carefully chosen to allow you to explore the area and its attractions. Most routes are circular or out-and-back, although some linear walks may be included that use public transport to get back to the start. Although there may be some climbs there is no challenging terrain, but do bear in mind that conditions can sometimes be wet or muddy underfoot. A route summary table is included on page 6 to help you choose the right walk.

Clothing and footwear

You won't need any special equipment to enjoy these walks. The weather in Britain can be changeable, so choose clothing suitable for the season and wear or carry a waterproof jacket. For footwear, comfortable walking boots or trainers with a good grip are best. A small rucksack for drinks, snacks and spare clothing is useful. See www.adventuresmart.uk.

Walk descriptions

At the beginning of each walk you'll find all the information you need:

- start/finish location, with a what3words address to help you find it
- parking and transport information, estimated walking time, total distance and climb
- details of public toilets available along the route and where you can get refreshments
- a summary of the key highlights of the walk and what you might see

Timings given are the time to complete the walk at a reasonable walking pace. Allow extra time for extended stops or if walking with children.

The route is described in clear, easy-to-follow directions, with each waypoint marked on an accompanying map extract. It's a good idea to read the whole of the route instructions before setting out, so that you know what to expect.

Maps, GPX files and what3words

Extracts from the OS® 1:25,000 map accompany each route. GPX files for all the walks in this book are available to download at www.cicerone.co.uk/1247/gpx.

What3words is a free smartphone app which identifies every 3m square of the globe with a unique three-word address, e.g. ///destiny.cafe.sonic. For more information see https://what3words.com/products/what3words-app.

USING THIS GUIDE

Walking with children

Even young children can be surprisingly strong walkers, but every family is different and you may need to adapt the timings given in this book to take that into account. Make sure you go at the pace of the slowest member and choose a walk with an exciting objective in mind, such as a cave, river, waterfall or picnic spot. Many of the walks can be shortened to suit – suggestions are included at the end of the route description.

Dogs

Sheep or cattle may be found grazing on a number of these walks. Keep dogs under control at all times so that they don't scare or disturb livestock or wildlife. Cattle, particularly cows with calves, may very occasionally pose a risk to walkers with dogs. If you ever feel threatened by cattle, you should let go of your dog's lead and let it run free.

Enjoying the countryside responsibly

Enjoy the countryside and treat it with respect to protect our natural environments. Stick to footpaths and take your litter home with you. When driving, slow down on rural roads and park considerately, or better still use public transport. For more details check out www.gov.uk/countryside-code.

The Countryside Code

Respect everyone
- be considerate to those living in, working in and enjoying the countryside
- leave gates and property as you find them
- do not block access to gateways or driveways when parking
- be nice, say hello, share the space
- follow local signs and keep to marked paths unless wider access is available

Protect the environment
- take your litter home – leave no trace of your visit
- do not light fires and only have BBQs where signs say you can
- always keep dogs under control and in sight
- dog poo – bag it and bin it – any public waste bin will do
- care for nature – do not cause damage or disturbance

Enjoy the outdoors
- check your route and local conditions
- plan your adventure – know what to expect and what you can do
- enjoy your visit, have fun, make a memory

ROUTE SUMMARY TABLE

WALK NAME	START POINT	TIME	DISTANCE
1. West Pentire and Polly Joke	Poly Joke car park	1½hr	3.8km (2.4 miles)
2. Newquay	Newquay railway station	2½hr	8.6km (5.3 miles)
3. Watergate Bay to Newquay	Watergate Bay	2hr	5.9km (3.7 miles)
4. Mawgan Porth and St Mawgan	Mawgan Porth Beach	2¼hr	6.6km (4.1 miles)
5. Park Head and Pentire Steps	Park Head National Trust car park	1¼hr	3.2km (2 miles)
6. Trevose Head	Trevose Head National Trust car park	1½hr	3.6km (2.2 miles)
7. Padstow and Prideaux Place	Padstow Harbour	1¾hr	4.5km (2.8 miles)
8. Little Petherick Creek	Padstow Museum	3hr	9km (5.6 miles)
9. Rock and Polzeath	Rock ferry slip	3hr	9.6km (6 miles)
10. Pentire Point and The Rumps	Lead Mines National Trust car park	2¼hr	6.3km (3.9 miles)
11. Port Isaac	The Platt, Port Isaac	1½hr	3.5km (2.2 miles)
12. Camelford	St Thomas of Canterbury Church	1hr	3km (1.9 miles)
13. Tintagel	Tintagel Visitor Centre	2hr	5.4km (3.4 miles)
14. Boscastle	The Cobweb Inn, Boscastle	2½hr	6.3km (3.9 miles)
15. Bude Canal and coast	Bude Tourist Information Centre	3hr	9.6km (6 miles)

ROUTE SUMMARY TABLE

HIGHLIGHTS
Coastal views, beach, wildflower meadows
Historic highlights, beaches
Cliffs, beaches and panoramic views
Wooded valley, pretty village, historic church
Rugged coastal views, Poldark filming location
Panoramic views, lighthouse, lifeboat station
Historic harbour, beaches, Tudor mansion and deer park
Estuary and creek views, obelisk, wildlife, historic church
Dunes, beaches, historic church with literary links
Prehistoric fort, rugged cliffs, coastal views
Fishing village and beach, film and TV location
Wooded riverside walk, wildlife
Scenic clifftop views, King Arthur legends
Rugged coastline, medieval field system, church
Historic canal, coastal and clifftop views

SYMBOLS USED ON ROUTE MAPS

(S) Start point

(F) Finish point

(SF) Start and finish at the same place

4→ Waypoint

~ Route line

MAPPING IS SHOWN AT A SCALE OF 1:25,000

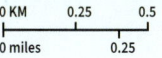

DOWNLOAD THE GPX FILES FOR FREE AT
www.cicerone.co.uk/1247/gpx

Wildflowers at Polly Joke (Walk 1)

INTRODUCTION

Watergate Bay (Walk 3)

Cornwall has been attracting visitors in great numbers since the Cornish Main Line between Plymouth and Penzance opened in the 1860s, followed by the expansion of the motorway network to Exeter in the 1970s. This is understandable given that the 700km long Cornish coastline contains over 300 beaches, many of them deserted and containing swathes of golden sand lapped by turquoise sea. The Atlantic Ocean encourages perfect surfing waves towards Cornish shores, making it one of the best surf locations in the world, with places like Fistral Beach near Newquay hosting major international surfing competitions.

The south coast is known as the Cornish Riviera, its sandy beaches and seaside resorts interspersed with quaint fishing villages, whereas the north coast is exposed to stronger swells, creating rugged cliffs and sculpting rock stacks. Inland, reminders of Cornwall's industrial heritage are ever-present, with the iconic silhouettes of tin mine engine houses dominating the skyline. As most mining activity in Cornwall has long since ceased, nature has regained these areas, and long-forgotten tramways and access tracks now provide easy routes through this unusual landscape.

TV programmes such as *Poldark* and *Doc Martin* and the imagery created by authors like Daphne du Maurier and Rosamunde Pilcher draw tourists to the area in the summer months, but those looking to avoid the crowds can still find refuge along some of Cornwall's less-trodden paths.

Along the South West Coast Path near Tintagel (Walk 13)

Walking in Newquay and the north coast

Walking on the north coast of Cornwall is breathtaking – sometimes literally when fierce coastal winds whip across the rugged cliffs. Winter storms rush past, carrying the scent of salt and seaweed, making each step bracing. Outside the main tourist season the raw power of the wind amplifies the wild beauty of this dramatic coastal landscape. Golden beaches nestle between dramatic headlands, with waves crashing against jagged rocks. Wildflowers adorn the coastal paths, and picturesque villages like Padstow and Tintagel offer charm and history when – and it is possible! – one tires of the beach.

The majority of the walks in this book make use of waymarked trails, often the familiar acorn of the South West Coast Path or yellow public footpath arrows. While there should be no real navigational difficulties, particularly on coastal sections where keeping the sea on one side is instruction enough, don't underestimate the undulating nature of the Cornish coast.

The walks in this book can be enjoyed year-round; the remnants of autumn storms leave the sea angry and tumultuous – perfect for a clifftop walk – and the crisp winter air hurries walkers towards welcoming historic pubs. Most of the walks are circular or there-and-back routes, and the linear walks make use of straight-forward public transport options. For many routes there are options to shorten or lengthen the walk as desired.

Things to see

Newquay is a lively seaside town famed for its beaches and surf culture. Walk 2 provides an excellent overview of the mix of natural beauty and buzzing energy that makes it such a draw to holidaymakers and walkers. Further west, the fishing village of Padstow has developed a reputation for fine dining, with an array of Michelin Guide restaurants dotted throughout the narrow streets. Walk 7 is a good option to walk-off lunch or build up an appetite. Cross the Camel Estuary on the passenger ferry to Rock – known as the Saint-Tropez of Cornwall thanks to its popularity with celebrity visitors – and follow the dunes to the laid-back surf village of Polzeath (Walk 9). Meanwhile Tintagel is full of myth and history; reputedly the birthplace of King Arthur, it features the dramatic ruins of Tintagel Castle set on top of cliffs with sweeping views of the Atlantic. Walk 13 is the best way to enjoy this atmospheric area.

Travel

The Cornwall Main Line from London terminates in Penzance, with the Night Riviera sleeper train from London Paddington a useful option. Change at Par for the Atlantic Coast Line branch line to Newquay. Buses do exist in Cornwall, but in common with other rural areas require careful planning. The number 56 bus runs between Newquay and Padstow and is ideal for accessing several of the walks in this guide. It's also a convenient way of facilitating linear walks along the coastal path such as Walk 3.

Where to stay

As the main transport hub, Newquay makes an ideal base for exploring the area. As expected from a popular tourist destination there is a wide range of accommodation available throughout the area, from basic camping in farm fields converted for the summer, to stately hotels and self-catering cottages.

South West Coast Path signpost (Walk 10)

Poppies above Crantock Beach

WALK 1
West Pentire and Polly Joke

Time 1½hr
Distance 3.8km (2.4 miles)
Climb 95m

This short circuit is at its best from the end of May to early July when the poppy fields are in full bloom

Start/finish	Poly Joke car park, West Pentire
Locate	///sprinkler.voters.spoiler
Cafes/pubs	Pub and restaurants in West Pentire
Transport	No public transport
Parking	Poly Joke car park or West Pentire Road (both TR8 5SE)
Toilets	No public toilets on route

On a sunny weekend, once the poppies are in bloom, this walk can be a little busy with visitors enjoying the deep red fields contrasting with clear blue skies. But it's worth the trip. This walk passes through the poppy fields before descending to the classic sandy Cornish beach at Porth Joke, its remote location keeping it free of all but the most determined beachgoers.

View across Crantock Beach to Pentire Point East

1 There are two car parks in West Pentire. This walk begins from the southern car park. Head back out under the height barrier and along the gravel track, turning left at the T-junction after the Gramophone Workshop. After the last house pass through the wooden gate into the National Trust's West Pentire Head nature reserve and continue ahead along the easy footpath to reach a signpost for the South West Coast Path. If you time it correctly, you may be rewarded with a view on the right over the red poppy field, blue sea, yellow sand of Crantock Beach and rocky Pentire Point East.

WALK 1 – WEST PENTIRE AND POLLY JOKE

Kelsey Head and The Chick

2 Turn right where signposted and descend towards the South West Coast Path along a narrow footpath between field boundaries. Turn left at the end, following the familiar South West Coast Path acorn. Ignore the path forking right and continue to follow the acorn markings. After passing through a vegetated Cornish hedge the views open as the path crosses the heathland of **Pentire Point West**. Follow the path as it curves left, offering views across Porth Joke to rugged Kelsey Head and the rocky islet known as The Chick. This path remains high above the beach – offering enticing views across this often-deserted sandy cove – before gently descending to a footbridge across a stream.

In the Cornish language Kernewek, *porth* refers to a bay, port or harbour, hence Porth Joke. Originally this bay was called Pol-Lejouack in Kernewek, meaning 'Jackdaw Cove'. Pol-Lejouack supposedly sounds a little like Polly Joke, which has led to this colloquial name.

3 Either spend some time enjoying the golden sands of **Porth Joke** beach, known locally as Polly Joke, or turn left along the sandy path signposted for Cubert Common. This path gently ascends, passing through an area of rough woodland to a car park adjacent to a campsite at **Treago Mill**. Pass through the car park and the wooden gate at the entrance.

SHORT WALKS CORNWALL

Poppy field above Polly Joke

4 Turn left, then left again to follow a footpath running alongside the campsite. Cross a footbridge then turn left onto the lane beyond. Follow the lane as it curves right and ascends sharply. As the gradient eases watch for a wooden gate on the left at a National Trust signpost. Go through the gate and turn right onto a footpath through the fields. At a gated path junction turn right and head uphill to reach the outward path. Turn right and follow the lane back to the car park in **West Pentire**. Please protect the poppies and wildflowers by staying on the clear footpaths. Don't be tempted to enter the fields, no matter how tempting the photo opportunity may be.

– To shorten

With your back to Porth Joke beach (Waypoint 3) turn left and head straight uphill to return to the poppy fields and the outward route. This saves 1.4km (30min).

+ To lengthen

Continue along the South West Coast Path from Porth Joke beach (Waypoint 3) around Kelsey Head to the wide, expansive dune-backed beach at Holywell Bay. This adds 5km (2hr) there and back.

WALK 2
Newquay

Start/finish	Newquay railway station
Locate	///silent.protected.spin
Cafes/pubs	Cafes and pubs in Newquay
Transport	Buses and trains to Newquay
Parking	Newquay station car park (TR7 2NG) or plenty of other car parks in town
Toilets	Newquay railway station and several around town

Time 2½hr
Distance 8.6km (5.3 miles)
Climb 160m

A walk around the UK surf capital, exploring long sandy beaches and rugged headlands – perfect for a stormy autumnal day

Newquay is known for its beaches, which are ideally oriented to take advantage of the strong surf generated by the Atlantic Ocean. Fistral is the best-known of these, recognised as one of the best surfing beaches in the UK and a mecca for surfers throughout the year. This walk explores the numerous sandy beaches and historical features that that make Newquay such a draw for tourists.

Headland Hotel and Towan Head

SHORT WALKS CORNWALL

1 From the square outside Newquay railway station cross the road and turn left along Cliff Road. Turn right as indicated by the South West Coast Path acorn symbol onto the Tram Track footpath, which provides a panoramic view over Killacourt Cove and **Great Western Beach**. Emerge from the Tram Track and fork right onto Bank Street, entering Newquay's main retail area. Continue through the pedestrianised area and curve right onto Fore Street, passing the historic Central Inn.

The Tram Track follows the route of an old horse-drawn tramway, built in 1849 to carry lead, silver and zinc ore from East Wheal Rose mine to Newquay Harbour, with coal travelling in the opposite direction.

2 Continue along Fore Street – still on the route of the South West Coast Path – then turn right onto North Quay Hill at the Red Lion pub. This minor road descends towards the early 19th-century Newquay Harbour. Once used to export china clay, iron ore and coal from the pits in St Austell, today the harbour supports a small fishing fleet and pleasure vessels. Before dropping down to the harbour, fork left past the Active Cellars building, ascend a flight of steps and follow the South West Coast Path acorns to the white Huer's Hut.

In the 14th century this prominent building was a hermitage where a monk kept a light burning to warn ships of the rocks below the headland. Latterly the hut was used by a lookout watching for shoals of pilchards arriving in the bay in the late summer, directing the fishing fleet with hand signals.

Continue along the footpath adjacent to the road as it curves around

WALK 2 – NEWQUAY

Huer's Hut

the bay to reach the rocky headland at **Towan Head**. It's worth the brief climb up to the small white shelter to enjoy the views back over Newquay Bay and onwards over Fistral Beach.

Below the headland sits the old lifeboat house, constructed in 1899 with a long slipway reputed to have been the steepest in the UK. The current lifeboat is housed in the harbour.

SHORT WALKS CORNWALL

Towan Head and the Old Lifeboat House

Newquay Harbour

WALK 2 – NEWQUAY

Fistral Beach

3 Retrace your steps along the headland past **Little Fistral Beach** and fork right, following the South West Coast Path signpost towards the neo-Gothic Headland Hotel. Designed by Cornish architect Silvanus Trevail, the hotel was built in 1897 and has entertained numerous royal visitors. Follow the path to the **Fistral Beach** complex – home of British surfing – enter the car park and watch for a path sloping up on the left. Follow this as it turns into a sandy path running above the dunes.

4 From this path, corralled between the dunes and a golf course, there are numerous opportunities to drop down to the popular beach at Fistral. Continue to the end of the bay and turn right to follow Esplanade Road. This road eventually narrows to a footpath, rounds **Swimming Cove** and climbs uphill to join the surfaced road at the Pentire Headland car park.

5 Turn left and follow Pentire Avenue as far as the junction with Pentire Road at the golf course. Cross the road to the bus stop and look for a footpath running alongside the golf course. Follow this to emerge at Atlantic Road. Follow this road to the junction and cross Tower Road onto Crantock Street. At the end of Crantock Street turn right along St George's Road and then left into Manor Road, passing the bus station. Emerging on East Street, follow this to Cliff Road and the railway station.

– To shorten

There are plenty of options to shorten this route; for example turn left at Waypoint 4 and follow the footpath across the golf course above Fistral Beach to return to Fore Street and the outward route. This saves 4km (45min).

Looking towards Newquay on the South West Coast Path

WALK 3
Watergate Bay to Newquay

Time 2hr
Distance 5.9km (3.7 miles)
Climb 115m

Start	Watergate Bay
Finish	Killacourt, Newquay
Locate	///craziest.light.result
Cafes/pubs	Cafes, restaurants and pubs at Watergate Bay, Porth and Newquay
Transport	Number 56 bus from Newquay to Watergate Bay
Parking	Parking at Watergate Bay (TR8 4AY)
Toilets	Watergate Bay, Porth Beach and Killacourt

A beautiful coastal walk from the spectacular surfing beach at Watergate Bay to the bustling seaside resort of Newquay

This linear walk initially makes use of the Number 56 bus from Newquay to Watergate Bay before returning to Newquay along a section of the South West Coast Path. The return walk along the cliffs offers no real navigational difficulties – just keep the sea on your right – allowing for full enjoyment of the rugged coastal views over the beaches at Whipsiderry, Porth, Lusty Glaze and Tolcarne.

Towan Beach and Newquay Harbour

Looking back towards Watergate Bay

1 From the bus stop at Watergate Bay, look for a narrow footpath running uphill behind the collection of shipping containers repurposed into food and drink outlets. As the South West Coast Path ascends, views open out over **Watergate Bay**, a wide expanse of golden sand framed by dramatic cliffs. The bay is popular for surfing, and you are likely to catch sight of wetsuit-clad surfers. The undulating path provides scenic panoramas over small coves and rocky outcrops with the opportunity to spot seals basking on the rocks below. After around 2km the grassy path reaches the steps down to **Whipsiderry Beach**, at time of writing closed due to a landslide.

> ⓘ *In Cornish, a pasty is known as an 'Oggy'. When cooked, the wives would shout 'Oggy, oggy, oggy!', and the men would shout back: 'Oi, oi, oi!'*

2 Go past the Whipsiderry Beach steps and continue along Alexandra Road on the pavement as it drops down to **Porth**. Cross the bridge and turn right onto the beach immediately before the Mermaid Inn. Despite the expanse of golden sand, Porth Beach is quieter than Watergate Bay and has a more sheltered feel. Hugging the wall on the left, cross the beach and ascend the steps at the far side to continue along the South West Coast Path past the public toilets.

The hamlet of Porth once stood at the entrance to a substantial river, with the tide reaching around two miles inland, and was the port for nearby St Columb Minor. Before Alexandra Road and the bridge were built in 1902, traffic used to cross the beach and ford the river.

3 The footpath rises to Lusty Glaze Road. Follow this past the hotel complex to reach the top of the steps down

WALK 3 – WATERGATE BAY TO NEWQUAY

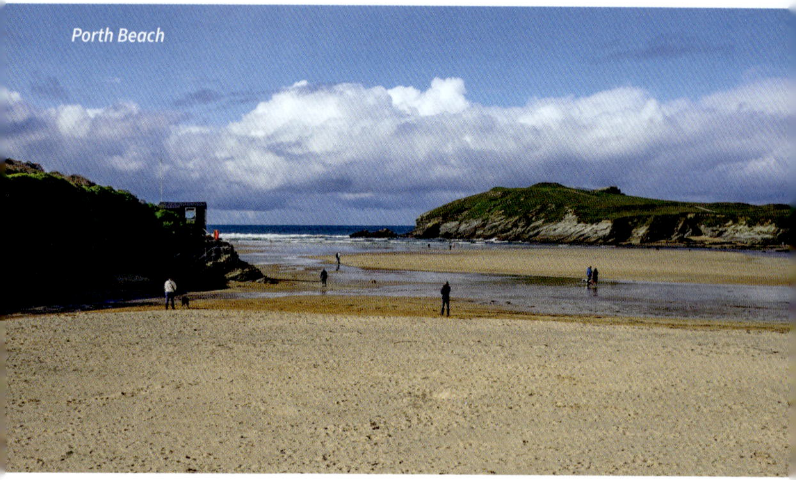

Porth Beach

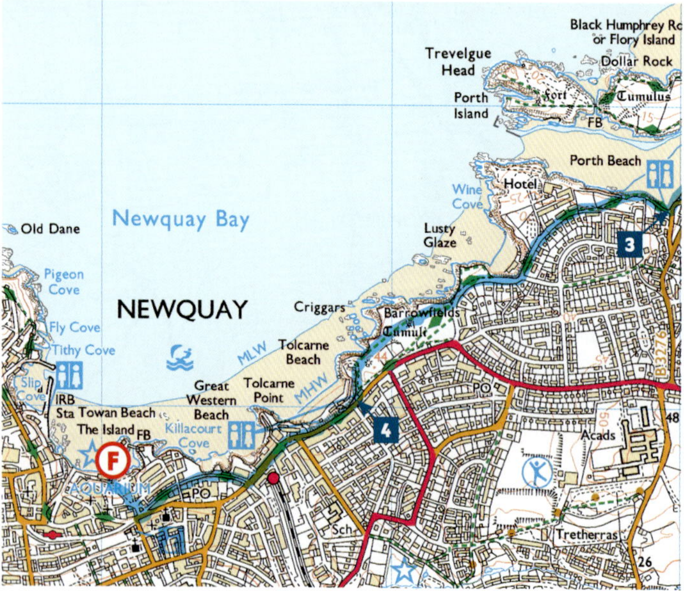
Black Humphrey Ro
or Flory Island
Dollar Rock
Trevelgue
Head
Fort
Tumulus
Porth
Island
FB
Porth Beach
Hotel
Wine
Cove
3
Old Dane
Newquay Bay
Lusty
Glaze
Pigeon
Cove
NEWQUAY
Criggars
Barrowfields
Tumuli
Fly Cove
Tithy Cove
MLW
Tolcarne
Beach
Slip
Cove
IRB
Great
Western
Beach
Tolcarne
Point
MHW
PO
Sta Towan Beach
The Island
FB
Killacourt
Cove
4
48
Acads
F
AQUARIUM
PO
Sch
Tretherras
26
B3276

WALK 3 – WATERGATE BAY TO NEWQUAY

to the privately owned **Lusty Glaze** beach, a popular location for weddings. Turn right and continue to follow the clifftop path through the parkland known as **Barrowfields**, with plenty of benches and superb views over Tolcarne Beach and Newquay. This grassy area derives its name from the three raised prehistoric burial mounds (barrows) that protrude from the ground here.

4 Rejoin the road at Narrowcliff and turn right, passing a viewing platform with ornate iron railings, and continue along the pavement. Pass Newquay railway station and turn right onto the Tram Track, following the South West Coast Path acorn symbol. Enjoy the view over **Great Western Beach** and emerge on East Street. Turn right then right again and follow the road down to the small park at Killacourt. From here there are views over Towan Beach to the harbour, as well as The Island holiday home sitting on top of a rock stack accessed via a suspension footbridge.

> **+ To lengthen**
>
> This walk could easily be combined with Walk 2 from Newquay railway station, adding 8km (2hr 30min).

Great Western Beach

Lantern Cross and St Mawgan-in-Pydar parish church

WALK 4
Mawgan Porth and St Mawgan

Time 2¼hr
Distance 6.6km (4.1 miles)
Climb 115m

Start/finish	Mawgan Porth Beach
Locate	///smuggled.trombone.invite
Cafes/pubs	Cafes and restaurants in Mawgan Porth, seasonal coffee shop in Menalhyl Yard, pub in St Mawgan
Transport	Buses to Mawgan Porth
Parking	Car parks in Mawgan Porth (TR8 4BA)
Toilets	Mawgan Porth and St Mawgan

Step out from the golden beach at Mawgan Porth through the wooded Vale of Lanherne to the pretty village of St Mawgan

Leaving the popular seaside village of Mawgan Porth behind, this walk follows the tranquil River Menalhyl through the wooded Vale of Lanherne on pleasant, easy paths to the picturesque village of St Mawgan. Perfect for an autumn day when the leaves are a riot of colour and the beach is deserted.

Descent into St Mawgan

1 From the sandy beach at Mawgan Porth turn left, past the bars and cafes, then turn right along the minor road to pass the pitch and putt course. Continue past the village hall and holiday apartments before branching left onto a bridleway through The Park holiday resort. Continue past the holiday lodges on a track to reach a junction at the far end of the resort. Go straight ahead at this junction onto a footpath signposted for St Mawgan to enter an area of woodland.

The River Menalhyl, or Dowr Melynheyl in Cornish, means 'river of the estuary mill'. This is based on the words *melyn*, meaning mill, and *heyl*, meaning estuary, and a number of former mills are passed along the route.

ⓘ Mawgan Porth has earned the moniker 'Cornwall's Hollywood by the sea' thanks to an increasing number of celebrities buying properties in the area.

English oak in the Vale of Lanherne

WALK 4 – MAWGAN PORTH AND ST MAWGAN

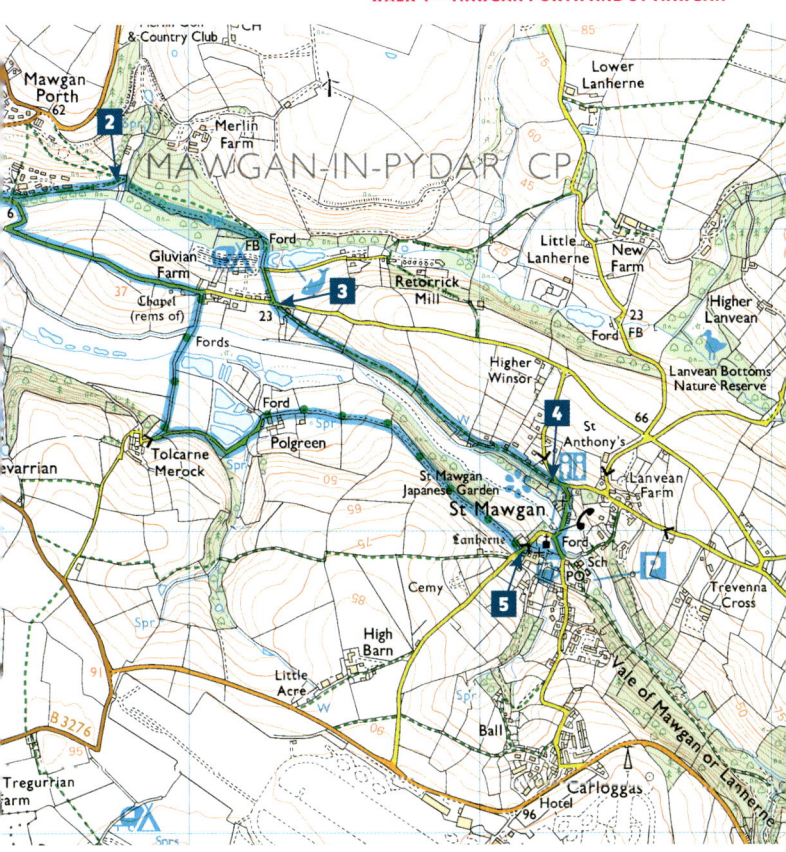

2 Cross the stepping stones and follow the wide path through the trees before the path narrows and reaches a footbridge and ford. Cross the bridge to reach a surfaced road by another holiday park. Go straight ahead, climbing steeply uphill to meet another road at the top.

3 Cross the road and follow the footpath through Menalhyl Yard, passing a seasonal coffee shop. Keep to the signposted path through the fields and into the wooded Vale of Lanherne. With dappled light streaming through the mature deciduous trees, this walk feels a world away from the

SHORT WALKS CORNWALL

Farmland at Polgreen

buckets and spades of **Mawgan Porth Beach**. Eventually the path drops down some stone steps and onwards to a surfaced driveway. Turn left and follow it to the public road.

4 Turn right and downhill to enter the village of **St Mawgan**. Pass the former Methodist Chapel and the village hall, cross the bridge over the River Menalhyl and turn left below the **parish church**. Before reaching The Falcon Inn, turn sharp right and into the churchyard of St Mawgan-in-Pydar parish church. Look for St Mawgan's well on the left and follow the path past the church door and up a flight of stone steps. Look out for the Lantern Cross, dating back to 1420, on the right. Exit the churchyard onto a minor road and turn left.

5 The building on the left is **Lanherne Convent**. Turn right through a farm gate into a field. Pass a row of stone farm buildings on a good track and go through a succession of gates, enjoying the views over the Vale of Lanherne. After 1km the track reaches a surfaced road at Polgreen Manor. Go past the buildings and follow the road past a collection of lakes.

WALK 4 — MAWGAN PORTH AND ST MAWGAN

Mawgan Porth

> ⓘ *Lanherne Convent Cider is made from ancient Cornish apple varieties grown in the convent grounds, in soil untouched by pesticides or fertilisers.*

Lanherne Convent is a cloistered convent, meaning that the Sisters never leave the grounds unless they need to go to hospital. The Sanctuary light has remained alight continuously for hundreds of years.

Watch for a track dropping sharply down on the right – signposted as unsuitable for motor vehicles – and follow this down into the valley. Cross two fords via footbridges and ascend to a quiet lane at **Gluvian Farm**. Turn left and follow this lane back to **Mawgan Porth**.

— To shorten

Turn right along the lane at Waypoint 3 instead of entering Menalhyl Yard and return to Mawgan Porth. This saves 4km (1hr 15min).

Boat keel above Porth Mear

WALK 5
Park Head and Pentire Steps

Start/finish	*Park Head National Trust car park, Porthcothan*
Locate	*///droplet.narrow.horseshoe*
Cafes/pubs	*None on route*
Transport	*No public transport*
Parking	*Park Head National Trust car park (PL27 7UU) off B3276 road between Mawgan Porth and Porthcothan*
Toilets	*No public toilets on route*

Time 1¼hr
Distance 3.2km (2 miles)
Climb 50m

A short circular walk to Park Head, recognisable from the TV series Poldark, with coastal views over Bedruthan Steps

Lovers of rugged coastal scenery will particularly enjoy the view from the cliffs at Park Head, with towering sea stacks and picturesque islands. Exploring the rockpools at Porth Mear Beach sounds like the perfect way to while away a sunny afternoon. Although this walk requires a car to access it (or a 3km walk from the nearest bus stop at Carnewas), it is definitely worth the journey.

Heading along the lane towards Pentire Farm

Porth Mear

1 Leave the National Trust car park along the lane at the far end. Ignore the footpath heading left through the fields and continue towards the cottages at **Pentire Farm**. Before the whitewashed buildings turn right and leave the lane through a wooden gate. Skirt the stone wall then cut downhill across the field on a grassy path to a gap in the boundary hedge. Continue downhill into the gorse-covered valley bottom. Go through a kissing gate and onto a footpath through the vegetation. This path follows the valley towards the coast, passing the remains of a wooden boat keel, to arrive at a footbridge on your right, above the beach at **Porth Mear** cove.

2 If you'd like to visit the rocky beach, turn right to cross the bridge, otherwise continue along the footpath, now part of the South West Coast Path. Ascend to the clifftops. You are now following in the footsteps (well, hoofprints) of Ross Poldark, who can be seen galloping along these cliffs in the TV series Poldark.

This section of coastal heathland is ablaze with wildflowers like sea thrift and heather in spring and summer. Birdlife thrives here and you may spot kestrels hovering overhead or hear the calls of choughs echoing across the cliffs.

The path is well waymarked with the South West Coast Path acorn symbol. Follow the wooden marker posts, watching out for a sharp left turn after about 1km.

3 Follow the path through patches of yellow gorse to **Pentire Steps**, so-called due to the huge slate

WALK 5 – PARK HEAD AND PENTIRE STEPS

outcrops above the beach. Both Pentire Steps and the more-famous Bedruthan Steps beach to the south can be seen from this point, separated by the arched rock known as Diggory's Island at high tide. Access to both Pentire and Bedruthan Steps beaches is currently closed due to landslides, but this doesn't reduce the enjoyment of the views over this stunning stretch of rugged coastline.

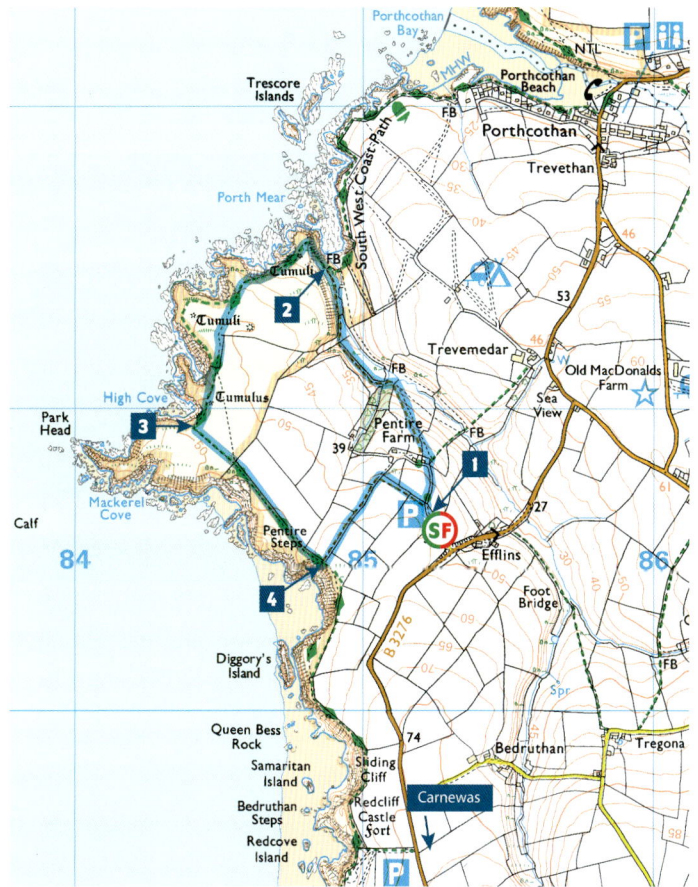

Trescore Islands and Porth Mear

4 Turn directly inland from the viewpoint above Pentire Steps through a wooden gate, signposted for Pentire Farm and car park. Cross the field to reach a good track. Before reaching the farm buildings enjoy a last view back over Porth Mear cove, the Trescore Islands and Trevose Head lighthouse (Walk 6). Turn right, go through the wooden gate and follow the footpath back to the car park.

✚ To lengthen

Continue along the South West Coast Path from Pentire Steps (Waypoint 4) to fully appreciate the sea stacks at Bedruthan Steps. There is a National Trust car park and toilets a bit further south at Carnewas, which is a good point to aim for. This adds 3.8km (1hr 30min) there and back.

Poldark

Filming for the second BBC adaptation of Winston Graham's *Poldark* novels took place in several locations in Cornwall from April 2014. This series, set in the late 18th century, follows Ross Poldark's efforts to rebuild his family fortune in a Cornwall largely reliant on mining. As well as a windswept Ross (played by Aiden Turner – no relation!) galloping along Park Head, several swimming scenes were filmed in the sea pool revealed below the Trescore Islands which lie off Porth Mear at low tide.

WALK 6
Trevose Head

Start/finish	Trevose Head National Trust car park
Locate	///clean.racetrack.bottle
Cafes/pubs	None on route
Transport	No public transport
Parking	Trevose Head National Trust car park (PL28 8SH)
Toilets	None on route

Time 1½hr
Distance 3.6km (2.2 miles)
Climb 105m

This short circuit is full of interest, including coastal views, Padstow lifeboat station and a lighthouse

This is an amazing walk, but it's difficult to access without a car. The striking headland offers panoramic views of the Atlantic Ocean, with rugged cliffs crowned by a historic lighthouse which has guided ships since 1847. To the north, dramatic cliffs stretch towards Padstow and the Camel Estuary, while to the south the coastline rolls toward Constantine Bay and beyond. In spring and summer sea thrift and heather add splashes of pink and purple to the yellow gorse.

Booby's Bay

SHORT WALKS CORNWALL

1 Leave the National Trust car park north, heading along the track towards the lighthouse at **Trevose Head**. There is a clear path. Before you reach the lighthouse leave the track to the right up a set of steps. The path curves right to go along the clifftop, with stunning views ahead towards the Camel Estuary and Pentire Point (Walk 10). On a clear day the Island of Lundy can be seen off Hartland Point. Follow the South West Coast Path (SWCP) acorn symbol through the gorse then follow the clear path to reach a large stone cairn. Ahead is

Trevose Head lighthouse

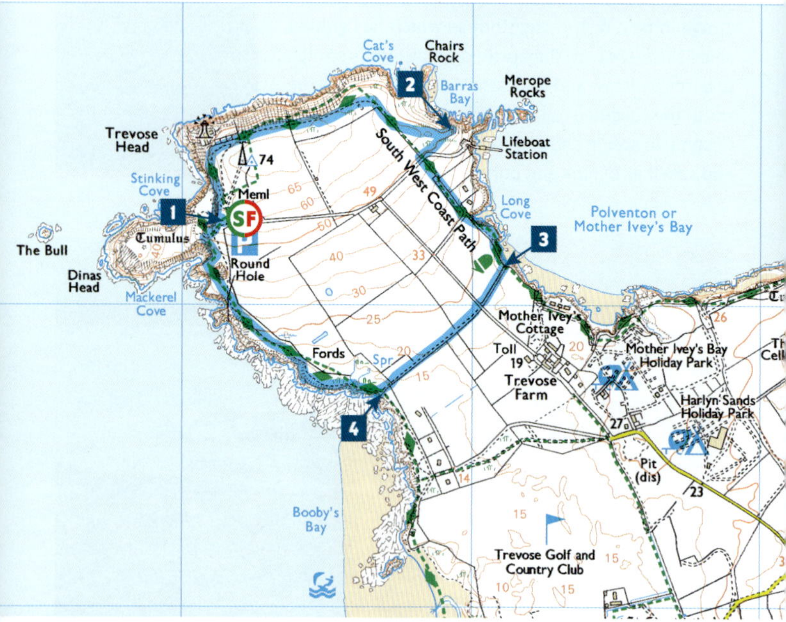

WALK 6 – TREVOSE HEAD

Heading through the gorse towards Mother Ivey's Bay

what must be the most scenic bench in Cornwall and an ideal spot for a break.

2 Retrace your steps a short distance and this time fork left to return to the South West Coast Path at a gate above the lifeboat station access road. Go through the gate, cross the road, and through the gate on the other side. The footpath runs between two fields, across another track, and onto the headland above **Mother Ivey's Bay** (Polventon). This viewpoint is spectacular, with jagged Merope Rocks to the north above Padstow lifeboat station and slipway. Continue on towards the golden sands but look out for a wooden kissing gate on the right.

> Padstow lifeboat station, established in 1827, has a proud history of saving lives along Cornwall's rugged coastline. Initially located in Padstow, the station moved to the current location in 1967 for better direct access to open sea.

3 Pass through the gate and follow the path beyond through several subsequent gates and across a track, with signposts indicating Booby's Bay. Traditional Cornish stone walls line the route. Eventually this obvious path reaches the rocky foreshore at the northern end of **Booby's Bay**. The sweeping beach of Constantine Bay beyond, renowned for its excellent surfing conditions, stretches wide at low tide.

Padstow lifeboat station

4 Turn right and follow the wide grassy path. Offshore, look for the rock outcrops known as The Bull – just off Dinas Head – and the Quies, a group of rocks around 1km further out. After a short ascent, the geographical feature known as **Round Hole** is reached.

Continue along the path to return to the car park.

Just past Round Hole is Dinas Head, between Mackerel Cove and Stinking Cove. Dinas Head is associated with the ancient Cornish word *dinas*, which means castle, fort, or prehistoric enclosure.

This dramatic natural blowhole was formed by the collapse of a sea cave, and the resulting massive chasm reveals swirling waves below at high tide. The large hole, around 25m deep, is unfenced and should be given a wide berth, especially in poor visibility.

Round Hole

WALK 7
Padstow and Prideaux Place

Start/finish	Padstow Harbour
Locate	///handbook.hurray.intrigued
Cafes/pubs	Plenty of options in Padstow
Transport	Buses to Padstow
Parking	South Quay car park (PL28 8BY)
Toilets	Padstow Harbour and North Quay Parade

This circular walk starts from the bustling harbour at Padstow before following the River Camel into the picturesque countryside and returning past stately Prideaux Place. It offers a perfect mix of a vibrant Cornish harbour town, historical landmarks, coastal and woodland paths, and sweeping estuary views above Harbour Cove. The first part of this walk, as far as Gun Point, is a designated Easy Access Walk suitable for sturdy pushchairs and mobility scooters.

Time 1¾hr
Distance 4.5km (2.8 miles)
Climb 100m

From Padstow's historic harbour to the Tudor mansion of Prideaux Place, with panoramic views over the River Camel

The Deer Park at Prideaux Place

SHORT WALKS CORNWALL

WALK 7 – PADSTOW AND PRIDEAUX PLACE

1 Begin from the northern corner of Padstow's inner harbour at the corner of North Quay Parade and The Strand. If you can secure a seat inside, the shelter here is a perfect oasis from the hustle and bustle of Padstow. Follow the harbour along North Quay Parade, passing the historic brick-built Shipwrights pub, and fork left onto a path rising away from the harbour. Ignore a path turning left and continue straight ahead along an easy, gently rising footpath. There are panoramic views over the River Camel Estuary to Rock (Walk 9). The path eventually reaches the war memorial above **St Saviour's Point**.

> ⓘ *Celebrity chef Rick Stein opened his restaurant in Padstow in 1975. His influence transformed Padstow into a gastronomic hub focused on high-quality, locally sourced ingredients, particularly seafood.*

2 After enjoying the view from here, continue along the South West Coast Path beyond on a compacted gravel track. There are numerous small footpaths heading down to the sandy beach revealed at **St George's Cove** at low tide. Follow the path as it curves inland into a patch of woodland, supposedly the site of St George's holy well. This easy, pleasant path returns to the coast and continues to the Napoleonic gun emplacement and fortifications at **Gun Point**. The path narrows here. Look out to sea for the Doom Bar – a sand bar that forms a dangerous obstruction in the mouth of the estuary, site of shipwrecks and deaths as recently as 2020. Continue along the path above the dunes and the expansive beach at **Harbour Cove** and cross a stone stile to reach a track running inland.

War memorial at Padstow

Above Harbour Cove

The Mermaid of Padstow is a ballad telling the story of a mermaid that fell in love with local lad, Tom Yeo, who mistook her for a seal and shot her. In revenge she called up a huge storm that wrecked all the ships in the harbour and threw a huge sandbar across the river.

3 Turn left and follow this track as it runs uphill through farmland, being sure to glance back and enjoy the views over the estuary to Polzeath (Walk 9) and Pentire Point (Walk 10). At **Tregirls Farm** leave the footpath onto a wider track, then continue ahead as the track becomes a surfaced road and begins to descend back towards Padstow. On the outskirts of Padstow, the road passes under a stone arch to reach the Tudor mansion of **Prideaux Place**.

4 Continue along the road and pass the house and deer park to reach a T-junction. Turn left and follow the quiet road as it descends past St Petroc's church and pleasant whitewashed cottages to return to the centre of **Padstow**. Continue along Duke Street and turn left into narrow Mill Square to return to the harbour.

> **— To shorten**
>
> Turn left and up the short flight of steps after the war memorial at Waypoint 2 and follow the path through the fields to Prideaux Place at Waypoint 4. This saves 2.1km (1hr).

Padstow Harbour

Prideaux Place

Since it was completed in 1592 the mansion has been home to 14 generations of the Prideaux family, thought to have arrived in Britain after the Norman Conquest of 1066. The estate includes around 40 acres of landscaped grounds and an ancient deer park, with fallow deer often visible from the road. The house and gardens can be visited during the summer months. It is particularly popular with Rosamunde Pilcher fans, as the house features regularly in German TV adaptations of her novels.

Prideaux Place

Camel Estuary

WALK 8
Little Petherick Creek

Start/finish	*Padstow Museum*
Locate	*///otters.fattening.shun*
Cafes/pubs	*Plenty of options in Padstow*
Transport	*Bus to Padstow*
Parking	*Padstow Town car park (PL28 8BL)*
Toilets	*Railway toilets (at the museum)*

Time 3hr
Distance 9km (5.6 miles)
Climb 245m

An adventurous walk exploring a quiet creek with a small gothic church and remains of a tidal mill enclosure

This walk leaves the popular fishing port of Padstow to visit the Victorian obelisk that overlooks the town and estuary. From here the walk drops down to the quiet creek at Little Petherick, which winds through woodland to a little gothic church housing a surprising secret. Return is via the ruins of a tidal corn mill and the Camel Trail along the line of the former railway. The footpath along the edge of the creek is often muddy and is underwater at high tide, so pay attention to the tide times.

Crossing farmland to Little Petherick Creek

SHORT WALKS CORNWALL

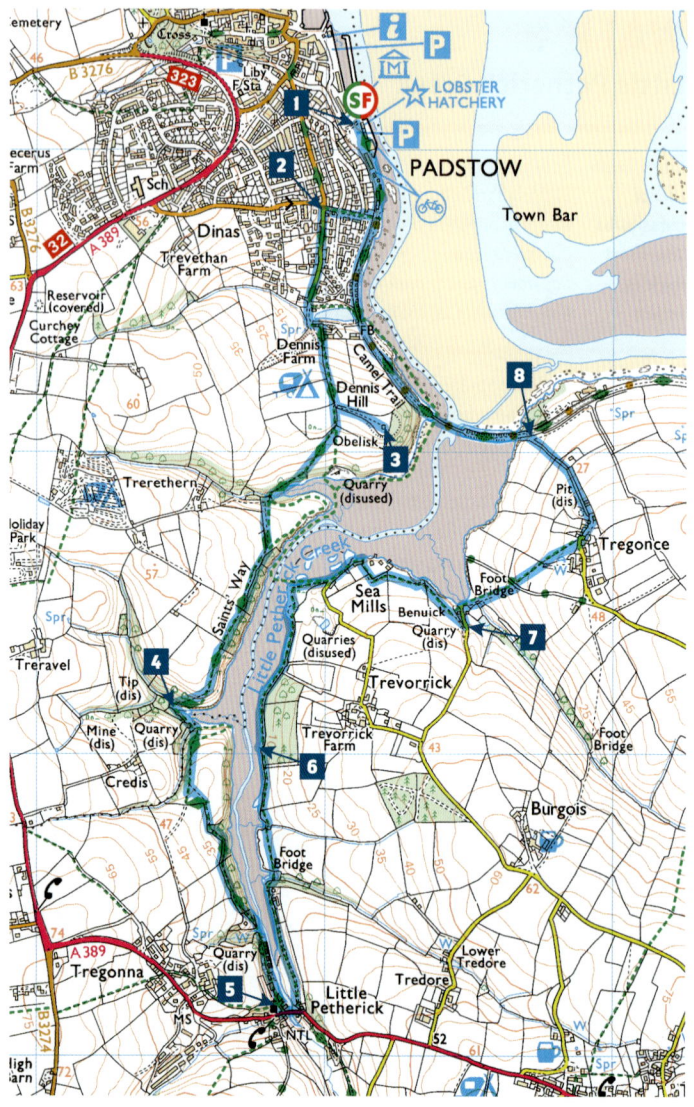

WALK 8 – LITTLE PETHERICK CREEK

1 Padstow Museum occupies the former Padstow station building. The railway to Padstow was opened on 27 March 1899 and closed in 1967. Leave the museum to pass the **National Lobster Hatchery** on the harbourside, followed by a huge bicycle hire facility and boatyard. This early section of the Camel Trail leaving Padstow makes for easy walking, with excellent views across the River Camel. Just after Padstow Sailing Club and Sea Cadets buildings look for a narrow path on the right climbing gently uphill to a residential street. Turn left and then immediately right, continuing uphill along Moyle Road. Take the second left into Dennis Lane.

2 Now on the Saints Way, follow the lane downhill, then follow the Saints Way signposting left and right through the **Dennis Farm** buildings and campsite, continuing through a farm gate into a field. Head uphill along the field boundary. Look for an ornate iron gate at the top of the hill and pass through this into a patch of undergrowth. Go past a building on the right to reach the prominent granite **obelisk** erected in 1889 to celebrate Queen Victoria's Jubilee of 1887. There are panoramic views from here back over Padstow and the Camel Estuary and onwards over Little Petherick Creek.

Dennis Hill obelisk

3 Retrace your steps, go through the iron gate and look for a stone stile on the left. Go over this, then turn sharply right downhill towards the creek. Entering the next field, continue downhill taking a grassy path running diagonally right towards a patch of woodland. A wooden Saints Way waymark post indicates a path entering the woodland. Follow this path as it drops into a quiet valley, cross the wooden footbridge and continue up the steps. Follow the Saints Way waymarkers along field boundaries and through numerous stiles. Navigation is easy, allowing for full enjoyment of the views over **Little Petherick Creek**. Drop down to cross a small creek via wooden duckboards.

Path alongside Little Petherick Creek

4 Head diagonally left after the gate and cross several more fields as signposted. A pleasant woodland path undulates along the creek before passing through a group of holiday cottages to arrive at the road.

> On the right is The Church of St Petroc Minor. The original 14th-century church was largely rebuilt in 1858, and despite the modest exterior houses an extremely extravagant interior at odds with its quiet creekside location.

5 Turn left along the road, carefully cross the **Little Petherick** road bridge and turn left along a track on the far side. Continue uphill until the access track narrows at the waterworks. Now on a footpath, follow this as it drops down and over a short footbridge. From here the path runs along and across farmland, with wooden duckboards over the boggiest sections. Watch for a signed path forking left onto a path directly alongside the creek at a footpath sign. This path is not accessible at high tide and is almost always fairly muddy. This path provides stunning views across the quiet creek, and birdwatchers will enjoy spotting herons, kingfishers, and other wading birds.

6 Follow the path, avoiding the wettest patches, to reach the remains of a tidal lagoon. The lagoon was created to capture the rising tide, the outflow

WALK 8 – LITTLE PETHERICK CREEK

View of the creek and obelisk from Sea Mills

being diverted via a large tide mill to grind flour. Reach the track at **Sea Mills** and turn left. Follow the track and look for a footpath on the right which skirts around the last house. Cross two fields and dip through a narrow gap in the hedge, down a short flight of steps, and turn right along a driveway. Go through the gate and turn sharp left along the road.

7 After around 50m turn right and cross the foreshore, go over the wooden footbridge and uphill over farmland. Cross a stile, turn left onto the lane then immediately right over another stile. Cross the next two fields to reach a lane at **Tregonce**. Turn left along the lane, wind through the cottages and begin a gradual descent towards the river. The **Camel Trail** is reached at the bottom of the lane.

8 Turn left and enjoy the easy walking along this popular surfaced trail. The Camel Trail recreational route makes use of 29.5km of the former railway, running from Padstow to Wenford Bridge via Wadebridge and Bodmin. Cross the three-span iron bridge over Little Petherick Creek, believed to be the only curved railway bridge in the UK. Continue along the Camel Trail to return to **Padstow**.

> ⓘ Since 2011 the Cornish pasty has enjoyed protected status, so a pasty can only be considered a 'Cornish' pasty if it was created in Cornwall.

Daymer Bay and The Doom Bar

WALK 9
Rock and Polzeath

Start/finish	Rock ferry slip
Locate	///little.reseller.kidney
Cafes/pubs	Cafes and pubs in Rock and Polzeath
Transport	Buses to Padstow then ferry to Rock
Parking	Rock Quarry car park (PL27 6LD)
Toilets	Rock Quarry car park, Daymer Bay and Polzeath

A ferry has operated between Padstow and Rock since the 14th century. The current Black Tor ferry operates year-round, runs every 20 minutes, and takes 5–10 minutes to cross the River Camel. This scenic coastal walk goes along the Camel Estuary, offering stunning views, golden beaches and wildlife-rich dunes, culminating in Polzeath's vibrant surf and charming village atmosphere. Return via St Enodoc Church – burial place of the poet Sir John Betjeman.

Time 3hr
Distance 9.6km (6 miles)
Climb 175m

Take the ferry to Rock and walk along golden sandy beaches, passing the wreckage of ships which have foundered on The Doom Bar

Rock ferry

WALK 9 – ROCK AND POLZEATH

1 Head up the ferry slip at **Rock** then turn left and through the car park. A footpath leaves from the corner of the car park and runs along the estuary. This footpath – part of the South West Coast Path – winds through the dunes, with numerous smaller paths dropping down to the sandy beach below. Remain on the main, obvious path alongside the golf course which eventually passes to the left of **Brea Hill**. At the southern end of sandy Daymer Bay follow the path across a little stream and onto the sandy path behind to a path junction.

2 Turn left at the junction along a stretch of wooden duckboards to arrive onto the wide beach at **Daymer Bay**. Turn right, cross the sand and go up the steps to the car park. Turn left and follow the South West Coast Path signpost towards Polzeath. The footpath is easy to follow as it rounds rocky **Trebetherick Point** above a series of inviting beaches and rockpools. Watch for the unusual purple-and-green-striped rocks below the path. Go over a wooden footbridge, pass a car park and campsite and arrive in the renowned surfing village of **Polzeath**.

3 Retrace your steps back along the coast path, recross Daymer Bay and go up to the junction at Waypoint 2. This time continue straight ahead onto a path over the golf course – signposted St Enodoc and Rock. The path is indicated with a series of whitewashed rocks; keep to this route and don't

Rock Beach

Polzeath Beach

stray onto the golf course. Follow the path through a patch of undergrowth and turn right, with the spire of **St Enodoc Church** visible ahead. Fork left and follow the path to the churchyard entrance.

> The wind has formed deep sand dunes around the church, and effectively buried the church between the 16th and mid-19th century, to the extent that clergy had to enter the church via a skylight in the roof.

4 Leave the churchyard, turn right, cross the fairway and turn left to a path running alongside a strip of woodland, well marked with white rocks. The path widens into a gravel track. Follow this ahead, cross a small bridge then turn left. Leave the main track at a white rock onto a small footpath winding across the dunes. This path is clearly marked across the golf course and maintains a straight line, sometimes on grass and sometimes on gravel tracks. At a T-junction on the edge of the golf course turn left.

> ⓘ *Cornwall's coastline is dotted with over 150 shipwrecks, a testament to its maritime history.*

5 Follow this path through the undergrowth towards **St Enodoc Golf**

WALK 9 – ROCK AND POLZEATH

St Enodoc Church

Club. Curve right just short of the clubhouse and car park to reach a lane. Turn left then immediately right and follow the road down to Rock Road. Turn right and follow this to return to the ferry slip.

> **– To shorten**
>
> Miss out the visit to Polzeath by turning right at Waypoint 2 and heading across the golf course to St Enodoc Church. This saves 4.8km (1hr 45min).

Sir John Betjeman

Sir John Betjeman was a poet, writer and broadcaster. He was Poet Laureate for 12 years from 1972 until his death. St Enodoc Church features in his poem 'Trebetherick', which focuses on childhood memories of the time he spent in the area on holiday with his family. Betjeman later moved to the nearby village of Trebetherick and became a popular member of the community. He died on 19th May 1984 and was buried at St Enodoc Church. His gravestone can be found near the southern end of the churchyard.

Looking towards Pentire Point

WALK 10
Pentire Point and The Rumps

Start/finish	Lead Mines National Trust car park
Locate	///ample.bonfires.files
Cafes/pubs	None on route
Transport	No public transport
Parking	Lead Mines National Trust car park (PL27 6QY)
Toilets	No public toilets on route

Ideal for lovers of coastal scenery, especially rugged cliffs, this walk passes The Rumps, twin grassy knolls forming the site of an ancient Iron Age fort, before following the clifftop path to Pentire Point with sweeping views of the Atlantic Ocean. Watch for swooping seabirds and easy wildflower-lined paths leading to vistas over Padstow Bay and the Camel Estuary.

Time 2¼hr
Distance 6.3km (3.9 miles)
Climb 235m

Magnificent cliffs and expansive coastal views feature on this short walk to an Iron Age fort

To the coast path

Cornish hedge at Pentire Point

The Rumps

1 Leave the car park via a kissing gate in the corner, signposted to the Coast Path and Lundy Bay. Follow the grassy path down to another kissing gate, go through and turn left, now on the South West Coast Path. The conical island called The Mouls is visible from this point, popular with breeding colonies of seabirds such as puffins, gannets and kittiwakes. The path runs along the top of towering cliffs overlooking Port Quin Bay. Follow a flight of steps uphill with views ahead to the twin peaks of **The Rumps**. Continue along this obvious path, ignoring a minor path heading inland towards Pentire Farm. The path eventually forks right and descends towards the first of three earthen ramparts.

There is evidence of a prehistoric cliff castle here, which would have had earth ramparts and a wooden gatehouse separating The Rumps from the rest of the headland. Archaeologists have found traces of roundhouses in this area and evidence of trade as far as the Mediterranean.

> ⓘ *The South West Coast Path, England's longest National Trail at 1014km, includes 483km of Cornwall's coastline.*

2 Go through the gap in the ramparts and spend some time exploring the headland. In the summer watch for seals, dolphins and basking sharks. Retrace your steps across the

WALK 10 – PENTIRE POINT AND THE RUMPS

ramparts and fork right, heading uphill to continue along the South West Coast Path. Ignore a path on the left heading back to the car park.

3 Continue onwards to rocky **Pentire Point**.

Look for a plaque on top of an outcrop commemorating the poet Laurence Binyon, who composed the poem 'For the Fallen' – often read on Remembrance Day – while sitting on these cliffs in September 1914.

Looking from Pentire Point to the Camel Estuary

4 The path continues towards golden Hayle Bay, the popular surfing beach at Polzeath (Walk 9). This easy path runs along vegetated stone walls alive with vibrant wildflowers in spring and summer. The extensive views from this section of the route take in Polzeath, the Camel Estuary and the lookout station on Stepper Point. Reaching the small cove of **Pentireglaze Haven** curve inland and take the smaller path heading left, signposted for Pentire Farm. This footpath passes along a narrow flower-lined valley to reach the road at **Pentire Farm**. Go through the gate and turn right, then follow the quiet road back to the car park.

> ⓘ *The Cornish flag, the black-and-white flag of St Piran, represents white lines of tin between dark molten rocks.*

− To shorten
Turn inland at Waypoint 3 and follow the path past Pentire Farm to the car park. This saves 1.6km (30min).

+ To lengthen
Instead of turning inland at Pentireglaze Haven, continue along the South West Coast Path to visit the laid-back surf resort of Polzeath. This adds 3.2km (1hr) there and back.

WALK 11
Port Isaac

Start/finish	The Platt, Port Isaac
Locate	///tags.looks.drawn
Cafes/pubs	Plenty of options in Port Isaac, restaurant in Port Gaverne
Transport	Buses to Port Isaac
Parking	St Endellion car park (PL29 3SG)
Toilets	Roscarrock Hill and St Endellion car park

Time 1½hr
Distance 3.5km (2.2 miles)
Climb 125m

Famous for Doc Martin and the Fisherman's Friends, this walk explores the quieter side of Port Isaac

The picturesque fishing village of Port Isaac is famous as a filming location for the popular *Doc Martin* TV series, as well as being the home of the sea shanty group the Fisherman's Friends. This circular walk begins and ends at the Platt, the wide concrete slipway above the harbour, location of the group's early performances. Head through the narrow streets into the farmland above the village and explore the quiet beach at Port Gaverne before returning through this historic village.

Fishing boats on the beach at Port Gaverne

SHORT WALKS CORNWALL

1 From the Platt in the centre of **Port Isaac** go past the lifeboat station on Fore Street and curve left into Church Street, heading uphill along a narrow, picturesque lane of whitewashed cottages. Watch for a footpath leaving the lane on the left just outside a cottage called The Crows Nest. Drop down this path into the valley. Follow the footpath past the waterworks, through the holiday cottages at Port Isaac Mill – keeping left to stay on the footpath – and back into the woodland to reach a fork. Take the left-hand fork here and cross the footbridge.

2 The path climbs steeply to pass through buildings at **Trewetha** and arrive at a road. Turn left along the wide verge, and as the road curves left look for a stile in the hedge opposite. Cross this and follow the footpath alongside a field, with panoramic views to the left over Port Isaac and the bay. Cross a pair of wooden stiles and drop down into the valley along a grassy path. Curve left through a field and onto a track which widens as it passes houses to reach **Port Gaverne** and its pleasant beach with a small collection of fishing boats on the

WALK 11 – PORT ISAAC

Port Isaac Harbour and The Platt

Overlooking Port Gaverne

slipway. There is an idyllically located 17th-century hotel here, with a restaurant and beer garden.

3 Turn left and follow the road uphill, enjoying the view over the bay to the rugged Castle Rock headland. Turn right to pass below the St Endellion car park along the South West Coast Path. Follow the track as it curves left, then leave it to the right along a narrower footpath. Lobber Point is visible ahead across the bay. Follow this easy path as it curves left above the sheltered waters of

Port Gaverne and Castle Rock

The Haven. From here there is a perfect view across the harbour to Doctor Ellingham's house from the Doc Martin TV series. Follow the footpath to Fore Street.

The *Doc Martin* TV series began as a spin-off from the British comedy film *Saving Grace*, and helped propel fictional Portwenn (real-life Port Isaac) into the public consciousness. As well as Doctor Ellingham's house, look for Mrs Tishell's chemist shop on Middle Street and Louisa's cottage on Fore Street.

4 Turn right along Fore Street as it descends towards the harbour, passing a series of small shops and cafes. Curve past the Golden Lion pub and return to the Platt. This no longer hosts scheduled Fisherman's Friends performances, but on a warm night with a favourable tide you may get lucky…

> ⓘ *Sea shanties are traditional work songs sung by sailors to accompany tasks on ships like hauling ropes or lifting sails.*

WALK 11 – PORT ISAAC

Above Port Isaac Harbour

✚ To lengthen
Begin the walk by heading up Roscarrock Hill on the west side of the harbour and follow the South West Coast Path around Lobber Point. Head back inland along the footpath to Homer Park and drop down to the footbridge at Waypoint 2. This adds 2.1km (1hr).

Camelford

WALK 12
Camelford

Start/finish	St Thomas of Canterbury Church, Camelford
Locate	///sniff.livid.safest
Cafes/pubs	Plenty of options in Camelford
Transport	Buses to Camelford
Parking	Church Field car park (PL32 9TB)
Toilets	No public toilets on route

Time 1hr
Distance 3km (1.9 miles)
Climb 45m

A short walk along a wooded path by the River Camel to the clapper bridge at Fenteroon, returning via farmland

This quick circuit of the market town of Camelford is surprising – an unassuming alleyway leaves the busy main street to join a tranquil riverside walk through woodland and meadows. The route has a real countryside feel, with little evidence of the busy road a short distance away. In autumn the dappled light streaming through russet-red leaves makes this walk particularly enjoyable. From the granite clapper bridge at Fenteroon the route returns via pleasant farmland with views over the Camel valley.

Riverside path in Camelford

SHORT WALKS CORNWALL

1 From the church, turn right along Victoria Road as it turns into Market Place, the main road through Camelford forming part of the A39 between Bath and Falmouth. This section of the road through Cornwall is known as the Atlantic Highway. Cross the **River Camel** for the first time and follow the pavement as the road curves left. As the road narrows at traffic lights, watch for an alleyway heading left signposted 'Riverside Walk'.

2 This inauspicious path drops down behind the properties of Market Place to reach the River Camel. It is believed that the name Camel is derived from the river's Cornish

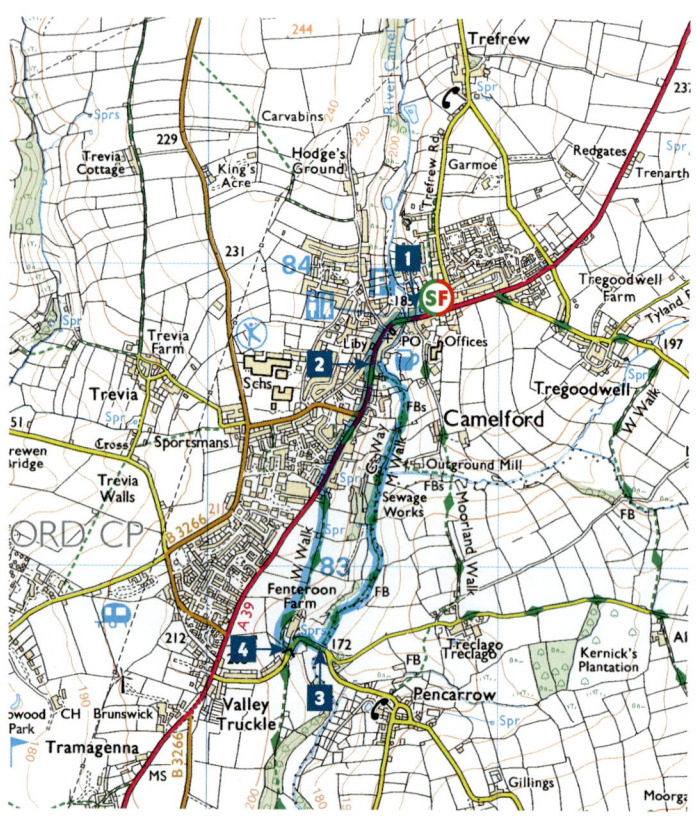

WALK 12 – CAMELFORD

Fenteroon clapper bridge

name Dowr Kammel, which means 'crooked river'. Follow the easy tree-lined path and cross the footbridge. Turn right along the bottom of a meadow, before recrossing the river at another footbridge. Ignore the next bridge across the river and continue to follow the footpath along the western bank. Now firmly surrounded by meadows and farmland, pass through a couple of kissing gates. The beautiful mature trees along this section of the walk provide perfect shaded picnic spots, and opportunities to observe wildlife such as dippers. The path eventually reaches the bridge at Fenteroon.

This granite clapper bridge is believed to have been built in the 17th or 18th century, allowing heavy carts to cross the river on their way to the market in Camelford. It's testament to the sturdy construction that it is still carrying traffic today.

3 Go up a few stone steps and turn right along the minor road. The road curves left and begins a gradual ascent. Watch for a short flight of stone steps on the right.

4 Go up these steps and follow the access drive as directed by a public

Camelford town hall and the golden camel weathervane

footpath signpost. After a short distance leave the track on the left through a kissing gate into the field. Follow the grassy path as it skirts around **Fenteroon Farm** and through a further kissing gate. The path crosses over and around several fields to emerge back on the A39. Turn right and follow the pavement down into **Camelford** and the start point. On the way back watch for the golden camel weathervane on top of the town hall.

> ⓘ *Cornish wrestlers wear thick jackets to grasp their opponents and make them land as flat on their backs as possible. The wrestler's motto is 'gwari hweg yw gwari teg', in English: 'fair play is sweet play'.*

Old Cornish legend suggests that King Arthur's principal fortress of Camelot now lies buried beneath Camelford, but despite being located in the heart of North Cornwall's King Arthur Country this is likely to be just due to the similar name.

WALK 13
Tintagel

Start/finish	*Tintagel Visitor Centre*
Locate	*///prude.confused.forgives*
Cafes/pubs	*Several options in Tintagel, cafe at Tintagel Haven*
Transport	*Buses to Tintagel*
Parking	*Tintagel Visitor Centre (PL34 0AJ)*
Toilets	*Tintagel Visitor Centre, Bossiney Cove and Tintagel Haven*

Time 2hr
Distance 5.4km (3.4 miles)
Climb 195m

An alternative, quieter approach to the popular Tintagel Castle, including the ancient settlement of Willapark

Steeped in Arthurian legend, folklore names Tintagel Castle as the place of conception and birth of King Arthur and even the site of Camelot. It's possible that this connection to King Arthur led to the first castle being built at Tintagel in the early 13th century. This walk feels a little counter-intuitive, initially heading out of Tintagel before taking the scenic route to the castle. However, it's a lovely approach and avoids the crowds until the very last section.

Rugged Trevalga Cliff

SHORT WALKS CORNWALL

1 From the visitor centre turn right along Bossiney Road, leaving the hustle and bustle of Tintagel behind. There is a good pavement along the road. On the outskirts of Tintagel at **Bossiney**, turn left past the Bossiney Cove car park along a footpath next to a communication mast. Go through the wooden gate and keep left, ignoring any paths heading right. Upon reaching the South West Coast Path turn left and up a short flight of steps. The secluded bay of Bossiney Haven below the path is incredibly tempting, but the steep path down is currently closed due to rockfall.

WALK 13 – TINTAGEL

Willapark headland

2 Continue along the narrow path and take the right-hand fork curving below a rocky outcrop. The path will eventually pass through a gap in a stone wall out onto the massive headland of **Willapark**. There are the remains of an Iron Age settlement here, and a pair of islands offshore known as The Sisters. The next section of the walk can be seen from here as it winds above the cliffs of Gullastem to the headland of Barras Nose.

3 Return to the gap in the wall. Turn right then right again to continue along the coastal path. Look back to fully appreciate the massive cliffs that form Willapark. Fork right, and keep right at subsequent path junctions, to follow the path over Smith's Cliffs and onto **Barras Nose** headland. The headland was the first coastal property bought by the National Trust in 1897, following concerns about overdevelopment after the hotel above the headland was constructed.

> ⓘ *The Cornish chough, a black bird with red legs and a curved beak, is a symbol of Cornwall, although it was extinct in Cornwall until recently.*

The cantilever bridge to Tintagel Head

WALK 13 – TINTAGEL

South West Coast Path heading towards Barras Nose

This point offers probably the best viewpoint over Tintagel Castle, with the cantilever bridge spanning the gap from the mainland. Look for the sea cave below Tintagel Castle known as Merlin's Cave, reputedly the home of the wizard Merlin of Arthurian legend.

4 Turn around and retrace your steps to the South West Coast Path. Turn right and follow the rocky path down into **Tintagel Haven**. This path is likely to suddenly get significantly busier with tourists visiting the castle and surrounding attractions. Once down in the bay it is possible to continue ahead and visit the castle (charges apply) – otherwise turn left and follow the wide path past the cafe, gift shop and toilets. Ignore the South West Coast Path signs turning right after the buildings and continue along wide Castle Road as it climbs back to **Tintagel** village. Turn right and follow Fore Street back to the visitor centre.

> ⓘ *The scones in a Cornish cream tea are served with jam first, then clotted cream – opposite to Devon's tradition.*

79

Tintagel Head

> ### – To shorten
> While walking along Bossiney Road, watch for a signpost reading 'To the Coastpath' next to a postbox and turn left along Back Lane to join the South West Coast Path at Smith's Cliff. This saves 1.5km (30min).

Tintagel

It is believed that there has been a castle on the headland at Tintagel since the 5th century, and luxury pottery discovered on the site suggests that this was home to the rulers of Cornwall. In the 12th century Geoffrey of Monmouth named the headland as the place where King Arthur was conceived, inspiring Richard, Earl of Cornwall, to build a castle here in the 1230s. The village of Tintagel has grown into a modern-day tourist destination popular with those interested in the mystical heritage of the castle. Now under the care of English Heritage, some of the castle ruins have been restored, and a dramatic footbridge built.

WALK 14
Boscastle

Start/finish	The Cobweb Inn, Boscastle
Locate	///hurt.affirming.hedge
Cafes/pubs	Several options in Boscastle
Transport	Buses to Boscastle
Parking	Boscastle car park (PL35 0HG)
Toilets	Boscastle car park

This walk explores the headlands either side of the picturesque harbour of Boscastle. Penally Hill offers excellent views over the village and surrounding coastline, including Pentargon waterfall, before dropping back down to the village then up to the lookout station on the headland of Willapark (not to be confused with the Willapark near Tintagel). From here you cross the medieval common land of Forrabury Common and visit St Symphorian's Church. The figure-of-eight route makes it easy to split into two shorter walks.

Time 2½hr
Distance 6.3km (3.9 miles)
Climb 340m

Starting from the picturesque harbour at Boscastle, this walk includes the old lookout station, waterfall and medieval farmland at Forrabury Common

Descending to Pentargon

Entrance to Boscastle Harbour

1 The Cobweb Inn occupies a prominent position in the centre of the village of Boscastle, opposite the main bus stop and car parks. Turn left and follow Penally Hill downhill towards the river. Don't cross the bridge over the River Valency, instead follow the riverside path towards the harbour. Pass the National Trust visitor centre and Museum of Witchcraft and Magic and fork right along a minor road above the **youth hostel**. As it ascends, this track offers excellent views over the harbour mouth. Where the surfaced road ends at holiday cottages, continue ahead onto a narrow footpath. Follow this to a path junction at a bench where the South West Coast Path forks right and uphill. Continue straight ahead. Eventually the path crosses a rock slab – be careful after wet weather – to reach **Penally Point**. The rock islet just offshore is Meachard, and across the harbour mouth can be seen the whitewashed lookout station visited later in the walk.

2 Retrace your steps to the bench and turn sharply left to ascend the steps, now following the South West Coast Path acorn symbol. It's a steep

WALK 14 – BOSCASTLE

climb, but eventually the path reaches a col. Turn left to climb **Penally Hill**, topped with a white mast, and enjoy the panoramic views along the coast. The cliffs in this part of Cornwall are particularly rugged and scenic, with a succession of sea stacks. Retrace your steps to the col, go through a kissing gate and continue straight ahead along an obvious, wildflower-lined path. This path undulates over two small hills to reach a viewpoint over **Pentargon** bay. If conditions are right, a waterfall can be seen cascading around 35m over the cliffs.

3 Turn right and cross a stile, then leave the South West Coast Path by turning right to follow a field boundary towards the road. Don't go through the gate onto the road, instead turn right and follow a permissive path through the field, shadowing the road back

SHORT WALKS CORNWALL

Pentargon bay and waterfall

River Valency at Boscastle

WALK 14 – BOSCASTLE

towards Boscastle. Go through two fields to rejoin the road at Hillsborough at the entrance to **Penally House**. A short distance ahead is a wooden gate on the right. Go through this and follow the panoramic path back towards **Boscastle**, emerging on the minor road by the holiday cottages above the youth hostel. Turn left to follow the road back to the river.

4 Cross the river at the footbridge outside the National Trust visitor centre. Turn right and follow the South West Coast Path signpost onto a road sloping up above the harbour. Leave this access track again on the left as it narrows to a footpath and provides stunning views over the harbour and Penally Point. The path curves left and continues along the clifftop to the sea inlet of **Eastern Blackapit**. Combined with Western Blackapit, a short distance beyond, these sea inlets almost cut-off Willapark from the mainland. Turn right and head through the wooden gate and out onto the headland.

> The lookout station here was once used by excisemen attempting to prevent smuggling and is now used by the National Coastwatch Institute and staffed by volunteer watchkeepers.

5 After exploring the headland return to the coast path. Turn right, pass **Western Blackapit**, and leave the South West Coast Path to cross **Forrabury Common**, known locally as 'The Stitches'.

> Once an ancient field system, this field was divided into 42 long parcels (each around an acre) in the medieval period. Each strip was planted with a different crop and divided by a balk – a raised bed of stone and grass.

Stone wall and foxgloves at Forrabury Common

St Symphorian's Church, Boscastle

Head towards St Symphorian's Church in the far corner of the common and go through the gate to enter the churchyard.

6 Spend some time exploring the church then leave by the main gate and turn left to follow a path sloping down to Forrabury Hill. Follow this down to New Road. Cross over the road and into Old Road. Follow this downhill, turning sharply left, to return to Boscastle. Turn right, over the road bridge and back to the start.

> ### − To shorten
> This walk is easily split into two shorter walks, splitting at Waypoint 2. The Penally Hill section of the walk is 3.9km (1hr 30min), and the Willapark section 2.7km (1hr).

WALK 15
Bude Canal and coast

Start/finish	*Bude Tourist Information Centre*
Locate	*///punch.conceals.erupts*
Cafes/pubs	*Several options in Bude, restaurant at Whalesborough*
Transport	*Buses to Bude*
Parking	*Crescent car park (EX23 8LE)*
Toilets	*Bude Tourist Information Centre*

Time 3hr
Distance 9.6km (6 miles)
Climb 175m

A pleasant stroll along the historic canal through Bude, returning via a scenic section of the South West Coast Path

The seaside town of Bude is at the very northeastern tip of Cornwall, popular with holidaymakers since the Victorians, who visited Bude for sea bathing. This walk explores the unusual canal – once filled with 'tub-boats' carrying sand inland for use as fertiliser – before crossing farmland to the coast. As well as their dramatic appearance, the cliffs surrounding Bude are of particular geological significance. Follow the easy path back to Bude, with its sandy beach and tidal pool.

Widemouth Sand

SHORT WALKS CORNWALL

1 From outside the tourist information centre cross the car park to the **Bude Canal**. Turn left along the towpath. There are usually lots of people enjoying the canal on a variety of watercraft – there is a boat hire station nearby if you'd like to join them. Follow the easy path, taking the right-hand fork at Bude Marshes nature reserve (the first Local Nature Reserve designated in Cornwall), which contains a large reeded area, important habitat for wintering migrant birds. The towpath continues on, soon leaving the outskirts of Bude into peaceful farmland. Before too long the path reaches a bridge – cross this onto the other bank.

2 Continue along the towpath for around 1.25km to a junction of canal, river and road at **Whalesborough**. Keep right, don't cross the river, and pass through a small car park to reach a track. Turn right, then left, and go through a wooden gate to follow a footpath heading uphill and then diagonally across a field. Join the farm track at the field boundary and follow this through farmland, enjoying the panoramic views over Widemouth Bay and beyond. The track eventually narrows to a footpath. Keep straight ahead, ignoring any paths branching off left and right, to reach the road at a wooden gate.

Bude Canal

SHORT WALKS CORNWALL

> The cliffs around Bude are made from Carboniferous sandstone, rich in natural fertiliser. This made the local mineral-rich sand particularly valuable, leading to the creation of the Bude Canal to take small tub-boats of sand inland for agricultural use.

3 Cross the road and follow the signpost pointing 'To the Coastpath' on the right-hand access track. Turn right onto the South West Coast Path. Keep to the path as the cliffs are particularly unstable on this section but take the time to enjoy the views back along the rugged coast formed from sandstone and shale layers. Follow the path around the headland of Lower Longbeak, bypassing a small car park, and onwards past Higher Longbeak to reach the road just before the houses at **Upton**.

4 Here you will need to follow the pavement for a short distance as the clifftop path has collapsed. Look out for an interesting tiny bookshop on the left while passing through Upton. Rejoin the South West Coast Path via a path on the left. Follow the path uphill across the maritime grasslands of

Crossing farmland to Widemouth Sand

The Storm Tower, or Pepperpot

Efford Down to the trig point at **Efford Beacon**. As you'd expect, the views from here are spectacular and this is a popular picnic spot. From here the grassy path descends and curves right to the **Storm Tower**, recently relocated inland from Compass Point and now overlooking Summerleaze Beach and the mouth of the River Neet.

The Storm Tower, known locally as the Pepperpot, was inspired by the Temple of the Winds in Athens, hence the octagonal shape with the eight principal points of the compass engraved on the faces.

5 Drop down the path above the breakwater and turn right, continuing

> ⓘ *The popular tourist attraction The Bude Tunnel is free to the public, stretching 70m from Sainsbury's car park to Crooklets Road.*

to a flight of steps leaving the path on the left. Go down these steps to the end of the road outside rose-coloured Efford Cottage. Follow the road and down a flight of steps to the canal sea locks. Cross the canal via one of the lock gates and follow the towpath

Summerleaze Beach

back to the start, watching for the sand rails on the left of the path. These are the remains of the tramway that once carried sand from Summerleaze Beach to the canal.

– To shorten

Turn inland after crossing the canal at Waypoint 2 and follow the minor road to Upton (Waypoint 4). This saves 4.3km (1hr 15min).

SHORT WALKS CORNWALL

Clockwise from top: Public footpath sign, Little Petherick Creek (Walk 8); Duke Street, Padstow (Walk 7); Port Gaverne (Walk 11); Wildflower meadow at West Pentire (Walk 1).

USEFUL INFORMATION

Travel

Transport for Cornwall
www.transportforcornwall.co.uk

Cornwall by Kernow (First Bus)
www.firstbus.co.uk/cornwall

National Rail
www.nationalrail.co.uk

Great Western Railway
www.gwr.com

Tourism organisations

Visit Cornwall
www.visitcornwall.com

Visit Newquay
www.visitnewquay.org

Visit Padstow & The Camel Estuary
padstowlive.com

South West Coast Path Association
www.southwestcoastpath.org.uk

National Trust, Cornwall
www.nationaltrust.org.uk/visit/cornwall

Weather and navigation

Met Office
www.metoffice.gov.uk

Windy
www.windy.com

Ordnance Survey
www.ordnancesurvey.co.uk

Further reading

Walking the South West Coast Path: National Trail from Minehead to South Haven Point by Paddy Dillon. Cicerone Press, 2021

Cornovia: Ancient sites of Cornwall and Scilly by Craig Weatherhill. Alison Hodge, 1989

The Atlantic Coast Express: The Bude Branch by David J Wroe. Waterfront Publications, 1995

© Phil Turner 2025
First edition 2025
ISBN: 978 1 78631 247 1
eISBN: 978 1 78765 212 5

Printed in Czechia on behalf of Latitude Press Ltd on responsibly sourced paper.
A catalogue record for this book is available from the British Library.
All photographs are by the author unless otherwise stated.
Cover illustration of Fistral Beach by John Bingley.

© Crown copyright and database rights 2025 OS AC0000810376

Cicerone's EU representative for GPSR compliance is Easy Access System Europe, Mustamäe tee 50, 10621 Tallinn, Estonia. Email gpsr.requests@easproject.com.

CICERONE

Cicerone Press, Juniper House, Murley Moss, Oxenholme Road,
Kendal, Cumbria, LA9 7RL

www.cicerone.co.uk

Updates to this Guide

While every effort is made to ensure the accuracy of guidebooks as they go to print, changes can occur during the lifetime of an edition. Any updates that we know of for this guide will be on the Cicerone website (www.cicerone.co.uk/1247/updates), so please check before planning your trip. We also advise that you check information about transport, accommodation and shops locally. Even rights of way can be altered over time. We are always grateful for information about any discrepancies between a guidebook and the facts on the ground, sent by email to updates@cicerone.co.uk.

Register your book: To sign up to receive free updates, special offers and GPX files where available, create a Cicerone account and register your purchase via the 'My Account' tab at www.cicerone.co.uk.